LINCOLNSHIRE

AFTER

BEECHING

An illustrated survey of some of the surviving railway operations in England's second largest county.

By Graham R. Jelly

BOOK LAW PUBLICATIONS

Saturday 3rd September 1977. Barkston East: The GNR somersault distant signal is 'off', awaiting a Saturdays Only train to Skegness on what was then a quiet stretch of line from Allington Junction.

(front cover) **Saturday 27th August 1983 Ancaster:** 20188 and 20173 roar through with the 0838 from Leicester to Skegness. The Great Northern Railway is still much in evidence with 'running-in' station signs and a then 110 years old Type 1b signal box. The English Electric Type 1s, latterly Class 20, became synonymous with the summer trains from the East Midlands to Skegness.

(rear cover) **Sunday, 15th July 1979. Sleaford:** All stop! Sleaford East's magnificent signals at the eastern approach to the station. There is one each for lines from Boston and Sleaford South on the Joint line. The right hand doll for each is for the Up main with distant signals for Sleaford West below. On the left hand side are signals for the line serving platform 3 which diverged from the Up main immediately west of the two-track level crossing, the distant signals for that route being fixed at caution. Originally, a third line, from Bourne, which closed completely on 28th July 1956, also converged here.

First published in the United Kingdom by
BOOK LAW PUBLICATIONS 2014
382 Carlton Hill, Nottingham, NG4 1JA
Printed and bound by The Amadeus Press, Cleckheaton, West Yorkshire.

Lincolnshire After Beeching

CONTENTS

Sunday 15th July 1979. Sleaford: A general view of the station in high summer. Engineering works on the East Coast Main Line caused the 0840 from Cambridge to Skegness to be diverted onto the Joint line and a reversal was necessary here. After running round, Class 37 No.37054 is backing on to her train but will then have to reverse back to Sleaford West to gain access to the Down main before setting off again for a day at the seaside.

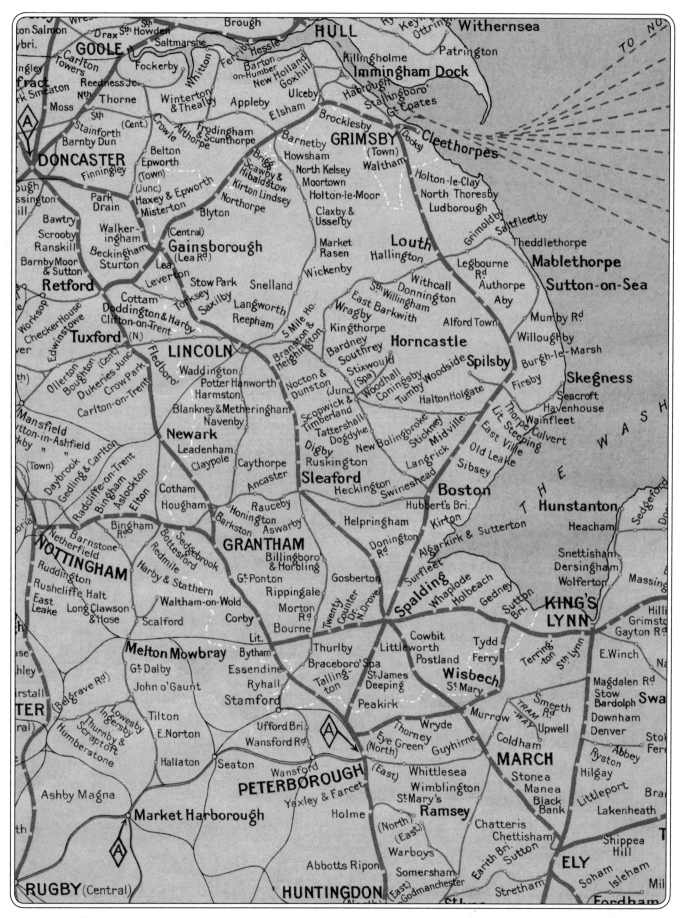

Lincolnshire's post 1974 inland boundaries have been superimposed onto this extract from a London & North Eastern Railway system map. Though, naturally, prominence is given to its lines, others are indicated by thin black lines.

INTRODUCTION

The idea for this book came when news was announced that the former Great Northern and Great Eastern Joint Line was to be re-signalled, involving the loss of many of the remaining signal boxes. I realised I had a reasonably representative collection of slides mainly from the 1970s covering this fascinating route. Further, living in the East Midlands it had become apparent to me soon after taking up railway photography in the mid 70s that there existed only a few miles to the east, in Lincolnshire, a vast treasure trove of attractive signal boxes, somersault signals and pre-grouping trackside signs on the route to Skegness. A seat in the front compartment of diesel multiple units had provided the ideal facility to survey these lines and note where the treasures lay, in advance of future expeditions.

The Great Northern Railway's line from Peterborough through Spalding, Boston, Lincoln and Gainsborough to Doncaster had briefly been part of the original East Coast Main Line from London to the north before the opening of the more direct 'Towns Line' through Grantham and Newark in 1852 considerably shortened the distance between Peterborough and Doncaster. The Great Eastern and Great Northern companies eventually joined forces after over 20 years of posturing and negotiations, which ranged from proposing rival schemes to complete amalgamation, to complete a more convenient alternative route from Cambridgeshire to Doncaster. This combined part of the existing route with a new line between Spalding and Lincoln. This, amongst other benefits, gave the Great Eastern access to the Yorkshire coalfield. As with several of its joint ventures, the benefits to the Great Northern Railway are less obvious.

In common with many parts of the country, the Beeching era had not been kind to Lincolnshire's railways and many lines had closed. Most notable of these were the former Great Northern Railway's lines from Spalding to Grimsby, Boston to Lincoln and Grantham to Lincoln, from Honington Junction northwards. After much lobbying, the railway to Skegness was reprieved, though the sister resort of Mablethorpe was not so fortunate. Thus, a section of the former East Lincolnshire main line, between Boston and Firsby had to be retained to in effect provide an extension to the Skegness branch.

This book does not dwell on the lines that were lost, worthy and fascinating though that story is. Instead, it concentrates on what remained in central and southern Lincolnshire, a county second only to Yorkshire in size. There was some small consolation in that for the most part, the live railways that survived echoed the character of the abandoned lines that were quietly returning to nature nearby.

On visiting the stations at Boston, Lincoln, Skegness and Spalding I discovered though there were vacant track beds and trackless platforms, nevertheless much still survived as if frozen in time. However, it soon became apparent that the process of rationalisation had not halted - it was happening here perhaps a little more slowly than elsewhere.

In 1981, BR singled three sections of the line towards Skegness east of Sleaford. Summer Saturdays in particular were still busy on this line but the tidal flow nature of the additional trains reduced the impact of the singling though, no doubt, causing some journey times to be extended. The impact on late running trains is best left to the imagination. Also in the early 1980s, Spalding was drastically reduced to a two-track corridor and the section of Joint line between there and March was closed completely in November 1982. No more would it be able to accommodate a large number of excursions for its annual tulip parade.

Major changes took place in Lincoln in 1985 to facilitate the closure of St Marks, the former Midland Railway station, by concentrating all services on Central, the more than adequate former Great Northern Railway station. The abandonment in 1982 of the avoiding line just to the south of the city had enabled this, as part of the track bed on the western side was required for the new link.

After this, the Railtrack era may have been responsible for a respite in the process of change. The early part of this century saw the elimination of the curve from the East Coast Main Line onto the Sleaford line at Barkston to end the need for local services to share the line between there and Grantham, thus freeing up more paths for fast trains on the ECML. A new east to north curve at Allington just west of Grantham replaced it, meaning local services now first go west from there, irrespective of ultimate destination, but more importantly, they are independent of the main line.

In 2008, the Lincoln area was at last re-signalled allowing freight trains to run slightly faster through the station and to provide facilities for more efficient reversible working. Prior to that, Lincoln (Central) had been one of the dwindling number of stations where traffic was still signalled by boxes at either end of the station. Fixed distant signals on the approaches ensured a cautious passage through the station for all trains, causing consternation for motorists and pedestrians waiting at the notorious level crossings.

The programme of re-signalling of the Joint line running from 2013 to mid 2014 spells the loss of many more traditional signal boxes. Unless otherwise stated, the signal boxes depicted were due to be victims of this scheme. However, even after this, some will still survive in the area covered by this book. The existence of so many level crossing means that their elimination will be a costly business to Network Rail. Nevertheless, plans exist to concentrate signalling on fewer and fewer control centres meaning the days of many of these, too, are surely numbered.

I hope this book will enable what has now gone to be enjoyed once again and perhaps provide encouragement for what remains to be cherished before it is too late.

Graham Jelly, Nottingham, February 2014.

Part One: THE GN & GE JOINT LINE - GAINSBOROUGH

(top) **Sunday 3rd September 1978. Gainsborough (Lea Road):** The peace is about to be shattered as 'Deltic' 55010 THE KING'S OWN SCOTTISH BORDERER approaches with the diverted 1000 King's Cross to Aberdeen. This train had left the ECML at Werrington Junction, near Peterborough, joining the Great Northern & Great Eastern Joint Line at Spalding, finally to regain the ECML at Black Carr Junction, just south of Doncaster. The signal box suffered fire damage in January 2009 and was not re-instated. *(centre)* **Sunday 3rd September 1978. Gainsborough (Lea Road):** An unidentified Class 47 approaches with an Up diverted East Coast Main Line service. The distant signal seen below Lea Road's starter is for Gainsborough Trent Junctions where the GN&GE Joint line joined the earlier former Manchester Sheffield & Lincolnshire Railway's line from Grimsby to cross the River Trent, immediately after which, the two routes diverged, to Doncaster and Sheffield respectively. The MS&L, subsequently renamed Great Central, received a toll for granting this facility. *(above)* **Saturday 8th September 1984. Gainsborough (Lea Road):** 40086, adorned with an unofficial, but wonderfully designed, self-explanatory headboard *CITY OF MANCHESTER HOLIDAY EXPRESS THE SKEGNESS WHISTLER*, passes having departed from Manchester (Piccadilly) at 0818. This was the penultimate occasion of Class 40 haulage for this popular train. Gainsborough will be the northern limit of the Lincoln Signalling Control Centre's area of operation.

GAINSBOROUGH-LINCOLN

Sunday 3rd September 1978. Stow Park: An unidentified Class 31 passes with the diverted 1204 from King's Cross to Hull. Having deputised for a Class 47, the Type 2 locomotive would be hard-pressed to achieve a respectable arrival time. The signal box is a GNR Type 1b, as was the Lea Road example seen earlier. It is now a Grade II listed building. The station here had closed on 11th September 1961. This was a notable date for station closures in Lincolnshire.

Sunday 3rd September 1978. Sykes Junction: Looking north, this was the junction with the MS&L's line to Retford going towards Sheffield. As an alternative route was available via Gainsborough, rejoining this line at Clarborough Junction, passenger services were an early casualty, on 2nd November 1959. The stub of this line west of the River Trent survives to serve the power station at Cottam but the retained section seen going off to the left was not to last much longer. The signal box, a GER Type 2 design from 1885, remained open until September 1988. This type becomes the standard box design on the Joint line for a stretch much further south, but here, was a Joint line accoutrement on what had originally been a pure Great Northern line.

Saturday 8th September 1984. Saxilby: A Class 105 Cravens DMU comes past, having just left the station with the 1026 from Doncaster to Sleaford. The signal box is an LNER Type 11 dating from June 1939, having replaced a GNR structure. The station is still open. *(below)* **Sunday 3rd September 1978. Kesteven Sidings:** Situated about a mile south of Saxilby, this box was of Great Northern Type 2 design, opened in 1891. Closure came in November 1984.

LINCOLN

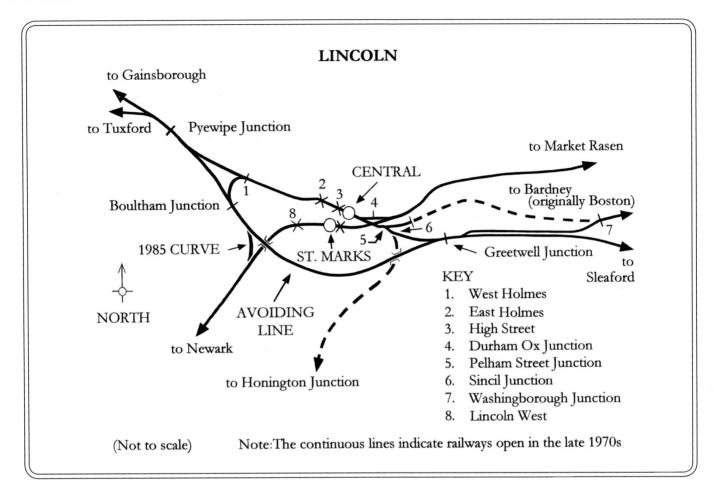

LINCOLN

to Gainsborough

to Tuxford ✕ Pyewipe Junction

Boultham Junction ✕

1985 CURVE →

↑ NORTH

AVOIDING LINE

to Newark

to Honington Junction

CENTRAL

to Market Rasen

to Bardney (originally Boston)

ST. MARKS

Greetwell Junction

to Sleaford

KEY
1. West Holmes
2. East Holmes
3. High Street
4. Durham Ox Junction
5. Pelham Street Junction
6. Sincil Junction
7. Washingborough Junction
8. Lincoln West

(Not to scale)   Note: The continuous lines indicate railways open in the late 1970s

(below) **Monday 18th May 1998. West Holmes:** A new road overbridge, carrying Brayford Way Lincoln, opened in 1997 and provided splendid views of the railway, albeit with a much reduced number of tracks. Looking west, a diminutive Class 153 working the 1152 from Lincoln (Central)) to Coventry fits nicely into the scene. West Holmes signal box, where the routes to Newark (from 1985) and Gainsborough diverged, is visible in the distance. There are Up and Down goods lines on the right hand side. The nearby Lincoln Signalling Control Centre took charge of this area in 2008. Four lines remain here, but the main lines are now more conventionally sited in the centre of the formation.

(above) **Saturday 2nd May 1998. East Holmes:** Looking the other way, a Class 153 is apparently adequate for the 1447 service from Leicester to Lincoln (Central). West Holmes' starter is cleared, as is East Holmes' home signal. Fixed distants on the approach to Lincoln reflected the low line speeds and the alert signaller in High Street will leave it a few seconds longer before lowering the barriers and clearing the signal into the station to minimise delays to the public and yet keep the train moving at line speed. This whole panorama would have been dominated by tracks in years gone past but the former GNR engine shed, latterly coded 40A, is clearly visible, albeit fenced off.

(left) **Saturday 21st June 1980. East Holmes:** An earlier, closer, view of the signal box, which was looking somewhat the worse for wear. This was at the time one of the oldest operating former GNR signal boxes, being a GN Type 1 opened in 1873. It was, unusually, of all wooden construction. The 2008 Lincoln re-signalling scheme rendered it redundant, but it now enjoys listed Grade II status. A change of location leading to a new use seems likely.

(right) **Tuesday 23rd Sept 1997. East Holmes:** Viewed from the car park, Class 60 60023, formerly named THE CHEVIOT, approaches Lincoln (Central) with empty 100t oil tanks for Immingham, the rear still passing under Brayford Way bridge. Clearly labelled East Holmes No.3, the signal has small route indicators in lieu of separate arms as previously carried. The choice of routes ahead was Down main or Down goods. This signal also acted as High Street's Down starter, or 'advance' to use GNR terminology, being signal No.10 in that box. The post also carries West Holmes' distant, applying only to the route along the main. In the left distance can be seen the former Great Northern engine shed which although greatly altered by British Railways, still retains the original walls. The shed is partly obscured by the huge brick base of the water tank (the tank itself long gone) which also served the shed, and the station water columns.

(below) **Friday 9th March 1984. Lincoln West:** A Class 120 DMU works the 1020 from Crewe to Lincoln (St. Marks) past the small Midland Railway Type 2a box, which dated from 1893. In 1912, the MR re-sited the structure a little closer to the crossing. This box had at one time had responsibility for sidings on both sides of the line, released by ground frames in addition to overseeing the level crossing. It was about ¼ mile west of St. Marks station.

Saturday 21ˢᵗ June 1980. Lincoln (St. Marks): 47426 departs across the High Street with the 1305 from King's Cross to Cleethorpes. The Midland had been the first railway to reach Lincoln; its branch from Nottingham opening on 4ᵗʰ August 1846. The Manchester Sheffield & Lincolnshire Railway's line from Market Rasen reached here in December 1848, making an end on junction with the Midland. In the distance can be seen the A15 Canwick Road overbridge at Pelham Street Junction.

(below) **Friday 8ᵗʰ August 1980. Lincoln (St. Marks):** Few trains can have run for so long, yet been photographed so little as the Lincoln Travelling Post Office Mails. A direct replacement for a stagecoach, the trains commenced in 1848 and lasted until 1991. The westbound train traditionally left Lincoln at 2000 and connected with the Up and Down *West Coast Postal* trains at Tamworth before the return working in the early hours. Latterly, and by then shorn of passenger coaches, the destination became Derby to combine with the Peterborough-Crewe TPO and return. Here the locomotive, 31194 and three-coach rake abut some other stock while stabled in one of the centre roads.

(above) **Friday 8th August 1980. Lincoln (St. Marks):** Lincoln's position away from the East Coast Main Line has meant that its direct services to London over the years have not always been satisfactory; in the opinion of its citizens. However, following the closure of the Grimsby to Peterborough line in October 1970, services ran via former Great Central metals and then through St. Marks to gain the ECML via the 1960s curve at Newark. There can certainly be no complaints about the motive power on this occasion as 'Deltic' 55015 TULYAR, seen arriving with the 1743 from Cleethorpes, is an upgrade from the rostered Class 47.

(right) **Wednesday 27th March 1985. Lincoln (St. Marks):** It is believed the Manchester Sheffield & Lincolnshire Railway built this distinctive octagonal box to control the crossing over High Street which enabled its trains to run into the Midland Railway's station. It was a block post until August 1960 but survives today as a sandwich shop!

(above) **Wednesday 27th March 1985. Lincoln (St. Marks):** A Swindon Cross-Country Class 120 DMU departs with the 1540 to Crewe. The association of these distinctive DMUs, whose front end had a hint of their GWR railcar ancestry, with this service was a long one. The MR Type 3b signal box came into use in 1903. Not surprisingly with only 20 levers, all were in use at its peak.

(left) **Friday 10th May 1985. Lincoln (St. Marks):** An informal but informative closure notice sited on a barrow on the penultimate day of operations at the station. Company rivalries lingered until the last, but few would have argued that it was not a move for the best. Discussions had gone on for many years on how to concentrate the city's passenger services on just one station and at one time, the odds were in favour of Central being the casualty, but instead time had now ran out for St. Marks.

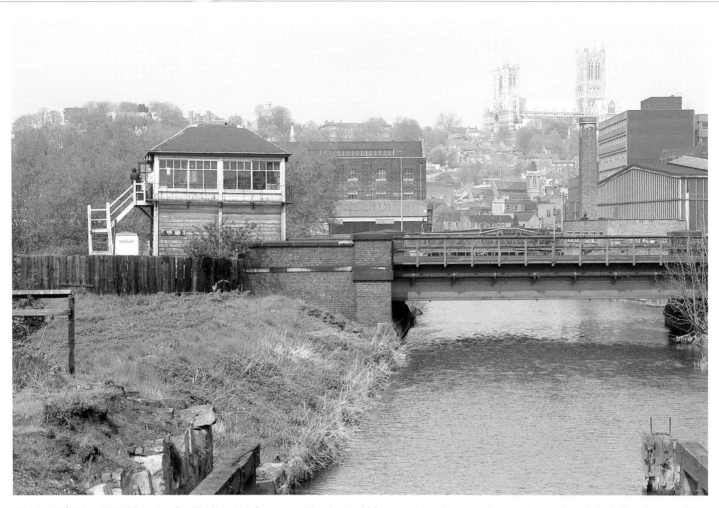

Friday 10ᵗʰ May 1985. Lincoln (St. Marks): No feature on Lincoln would be complete without a photograph prominently including the magnificent cathedral. In the foreground is the station box at St. Marks which, by sharp contrast, would be redundant in a little over 24 hours! The River Witham flows beneath the lines.

(below) **Friday 10ᵗʰ May 1985. Lincoln:** The new curve, to be brought into use during the following weekend, as seen from a passing train. All trace of the embankment of the avoiding line, which crossed over the former MR line, had been removed. This was fundamental to the creation of the new link. A Sunday possession will take care of the remaining track work and commissioning.

Friday 10th May 1985. Lincoln (St. Marks): The signalman was very gracious in the circumstances and allowed the assembled photographers to have a few unofficial vantage points. The top of the signal box steps provides a good view of a Class 114 DMU arriving with the 1447 service from Nottingham.

Friday 10th May 1985. Lincoln (St. Marks): A general view of the station. Class 31 No.31438 occupies one of the centre roads, latterly truncated to sidings. Though a through station, many services from the west terminated here, as illustrated by the DMU, echoing its origins as a terminal station. The track work and signalling allowed west bound departures from both platforms. The station originally had a twin bay overall roof but BR removed this in 1957. Shelter for intending passengers on the Up side was basic to say the least.

(above) **Wednesday 13th November 1985. Lincoln (St. Marks):** The view from High Street six months after closure of the station. Additional words seem unnecessary.

(right) **Friday 9th March 1984. Lincoln High Street:** One of a few pairs of Eastern Region blue enamel station direction signs marking out the route between the two stations. The stations were originally distinguished by their respective owning company's names the suffixes came later. Part of the footbridge over the railway, just west of Central station, is visible.

(above) **Sunday 18th September 1977. Lincoln (Central):** 'Deltic' 55004 QUEEN'S OWN HIGHLANDER passing through with the 1000 express from King's Cross. The Eastern Region 'running-in' signs were still a welcome sight at that time. Central was almost a backwater in the late 1970s, as the services using it had dwindled. The 1965 closure of the line toward Grantham via Honington and the re-routing of the Cleethorpes to London services via St Marks in 1970 had relegated it to secondary status. However, the place came alive on days of East Coast Main Line diversions, with such Type 5 motive power being the highlight.

(left) **Sunday 13th August 1978. Lincoln (Central):** 'Deltic' 55015 TULYAR, on railtour duty, is now heading for Skegness after changing direction in Lincoln. The tour had travelled from King's Cross via the Joint line, as we will see again later. This was also a 'diversion day' with regular Deltic hauled trains passing through too. Adding a touch of normality, a Metropolitan-Cammell Class 101 DMU stands in platform 6. At its peak, the station had no less than four east facing bays in addition to four through platforms.

Tuesday 28th November 1978. Lincoln (Central): High Street crossing seen on a frosty night. Whether by night or day, the signal box is an integral part of the scene; so much so that it has been given Grade II listed status in recognition of its value to the local area.

(below) **Saturday 21st June 1980. Lincoln (Central):** 37025 passing through on the Up main line with the 0835 Newcastle to Yarmouth. The main building, with distinctive tower and dating from the station's opening in 1848, dominates this view.

Saturday 21st June 1980. Lincoln (Central): Viewed from the late and much lamented footbridge at High Street, 37054 is preparing to depart from Platform 6 with a summer Saturday extra. This vantage point provided an excellent view of the GN High Street signal box, dating from 1874, and its matching extension which was added in 1925 to facilitate control of the extremely busy level crossing.

Wednesday 13th November 1985. Lincoln (Central): Following the transfer of the former St. Marks services in May 1985, Central, at a stroke became a much busier station, more befitting its capacity, facilities and location a little nearer the city centre. A Swindon Cross-Country Class 120 DMU leaves with the 1232 service to Crewe as a Class 101 DMU arrives with the 1210 working from Newark (Northgate) to Cleethorpes. The signallers at High Street consequently became much busier and would welcome 'two for one' opportunities like this.

(above) **Wednesday 13th November 1985. Lincoln (Central):** 31177 passing through on the Down main with a ballast train comprising a rake of 40t Ballast Hoppers flanked by two 20t Shark Plough Brakes.

(below) **Wednesday 13th November 1985. Lincoln (Central):** Seen from the A15 Canwick Road bridge, and with shadows lengthening, a four car DMU leaves with the 1400 from Newark (Northgate) to Cleethorpes. 31187, seen earlier, now stables in the bay Platform 2.

Tuesday April 1st 1986. Lincoln (Central): A Class 101 DMU arrives at Platform 5 with the 1226 working from Doncaster to Cambridge. Within seconds, the relentless flow of traffic along High Street will be able to re-commence - for a few minutes at least. Platforms 5 and 6 originally had substantial roofs, which extended over the platform lines supported by stanchions between the respective platform and main lines. High Street's No.2 signal on the Down main, with white board to aid sighting, dominates the foreground. Its design was a legacy to the days of the roof, as a conventionally post-mounted signal arm would not have been visible.

Tuesday 11th March 1986. Lincoln (Central): A drab day which at least offered the chance to photograph 47055, heading along the Up main with a train of oil tanker empties for Immingham, without excessive shadow obscuring detail on Platform 6. The new order in the form of a recently introduced Class 150 Sprinter is on Platform 4. These had replaced the Class 120 DMUs on the service from the Nottingham line; their frequent appearances at Central consequently confined to little more than six months. *(below)* **Tuesday April 1st 1986. Lincoln (Central):** A Class 150 on arrival at Platform 5 with the 1120 service from Crewe. This unit would have to proceed to Pelham Street Junction at the east end before re-entering the station on either platform 6 or 7 to form the return working. It was to be another 22 years before re-signalling enabled the greater efficiency of reversible working from the platforms. The station footbridge is Grade II listed along with the station building.

(above) **Wednesday 13th November 1985. Lincoln (Central):** A Derby-built Class 114 DMU leaves Platform 7 with the 1230 service to Nottingham. The station was able to cope with the increased level of services without the erstwhile Platform 8, seen on the right hand side, which had lost its track many years previously. The footbridge which crossed the lines at this point had by now been demolished.

(opposite, top) **Tuesday April 1st 1986. Lincoln (Central):** A four car Class 114 DMU set heads off towards the carriage sidings and maintenance facilities beyond the east end of the station. The phasing out of these units, which had been such stalwarts of Lincolnshire's local services for many years, was gradual as the second-generation DMU era dawned.

(left) **Tuesday 23rd Sept 1997. Lincoln (Central):** The adjacent car park offered the opportunity for a close up view of the signals controlling entry to the station from the west. On the right, High Street's No.35 was for the Up main, with a fixed distant for Pelham Street Junction below. Signal No.33 was to Platform 5 and the calling on arm below (No.34) gave authority to proceed into the platform when already occupied. Originally, there had been a calling on arm for the Up Main too. By now, lifting barriers had replaced the crossing gates. The footbridge at High Street had been removed to the continuing consternation of the local population.

(opposite) **Thursday, 17th November 2005. Lincoln (Central):** Class 66 No.66250 takes a westbound freight along the Down main. Happily, the semaphores had lasted into the 21st century. High Street signal box had gained new name boards more sympathetic to the originals. As with the other local boxes, it finally closed under the Lincoln re-signalling scheme on 19th July 2008.

Sunday, 18th September 1977. Pelham Street Junction: 'Deltic' 55006 THE FIFE & FORFAR YEOMANRY passes with a diverted northbound ECML express. In the foreground is the level crossing of the GN line and, left to right, the MS&L's line from north Lincolnshire. These two lines were connected by the spur seen on the left; the meeting of the two Company's lines being called Durham Ox Junction. From March 1906, the GC totally ceased use of the MR station in favour of the GN station, via this spur. Until 1958, Durham Ox road level crossing used to cross the lines in the immediate foreground. In the middle distance is the erstwhile left hand divergence towards Boston, a very short stub of which survived to serve a freight terminal. In the far middle distance, the embankment of the GN&GE avoiding line is visible below the dark trees.

Sunday 26th June 1977. Pelham Street Junction: A telephoto view shows the kink in the line at Sincil Junction adjacent to Sincil Bank signal box. This curve was the start of the Honington line, opened in 1867 and preceded the Joint line (ahead) by fifteen years, diverging to the right behind the fence. Though exaggerated in this view, the curve was severe enough to warrant a 15 m.p.h. speed limit. In June 1962, there was a fatal accident here when a diverted northbound ECML express hauled by an EE Type 4 diesel took the curve at 55 m.p.h., derailing eight of its ten coaches. The locomotive stayed on the rails and came to a halt on the Down main just into the station. Sadly, the accident claimed the lives of two passengers and a sleeping car attendant. The track was slewed in 1984 to ease the curve. *(below)* **Sunday, 26th June 1977. Sincil Bank:** A wide angle view looking west. The doll for the signal on to the erstwhile line to Honington is clearly visible. The signal box was 184 yards east of Pelham Street Junction seen just below the A15 bridge. Sincil Bank closed in January 1984. It took its name from a footpath, which later became a road running alongside the ancient Sincil Dyke or Drain.

Sunday, 26th June 1977. Pelham Street Junction: A telephoto view looking west from Sincil Bank level crossing. The signal box was a GN Type 1, dating from 1874, which closed on 19th July 2008. On the right is the line coming in from north of the county with the bracket signal showing the choice of routes: straight on to St. Marks, or off to the right for Central. The signal in the centre of the picture (No.62) applied to both routes into the station having a route indicator to inform drivers which line they were to take in the station. High Street's fixed distant is below and below that is a calling on arm for when a designated platform line was already occupied.

Friday, 10th May 1985. Pelham Street Junction: 31459 with the 1335 Cleethorpes to Newark (North Gate) working has just cleared the flat crossing on the approach to St. Marks on the penultimate day of this route. The sidings for a coal concentration facility are on the right.

(below) **Wednesday, 13th November 1985. Pelham Street Junction:** Six months after the demise of St. Marks station, a Class 114 DMU forming the 1315 service from Cleethorpes to Newark (Northgate) approaches Central station. BR retained a single track over the flat crossing to serve the nearby coal depot that lingered on for a few more years and a miniature arm on the bracket signal replaced the previous full size version.

THE GN & GE JOINT LINE – LINCOLN-SPALDING

Sunday, 5th November 1978. Potterhanworth: We are now on the jointly built section of the route as 47543 passes with the diverted 0915 Bradford (Exchange) to King's Cross express. Potterhanworth was approximately 6 miles southeast of Lincoln. The typical GN Type 1b signal box closed in March 1996. *(below)* **Sunday, 5th November 1978. Potterhanworth:** 'Deltic' 55011 THE ROYAL NORTHUMBERLAND FUSILIERS powers past with the 1040 King's Cross to Leeds service. There were still a few traces of the station here, which had been a pre-Beeching victim, closing on 2nd May 1955.

(right) **Sunday, 5ᵗʰ November 1978. Metheringham:** Another 'Deltic' 55002 THE KING'S OWN YORKSHIRE LIGHT INFANTRY brings the 1150 express from Leeds to King's Cross through the re-opened station. As 'Blankney and Metheringham', the station had closed on 11ᵗʰ September 1961 but with new, wooden, platforms it rejoined the national network on 6ᵗʰ October 1975.

(below) **Sunday, 5ᵗʰ November 1978. Metheringham:** HST 254019 comes north past the signal box, named Blankney, with the 1200 service from King's Cross to Edinburgh. The LNER built the signal box in 1929, but to a GNR 4b design.

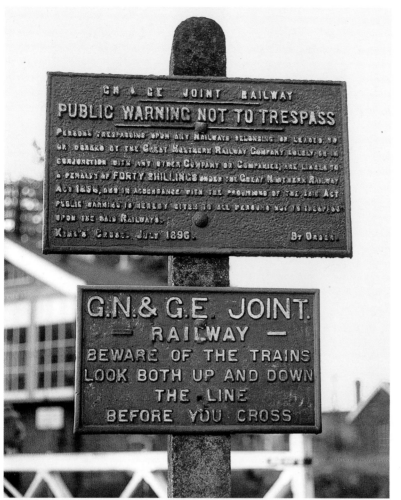

(left) **Sunday, 5th November 1978. Metheringham:** The GNR was responsible for maintenance of the line north of Sleaford and one lasting indicator of this was in signage. Here are standard GNR pattern signs, amended to show the joint ownership.

(below) **Sunday, 26th May 2013. Scopwick:** The LNER Type 11A signal box here opened in 1938. A station was also located here and named Scopwick and Timberland being midway between the two distant villages, but perhaps being convenient for neither had closed on 7th November 1955. In common with many signal boxes in recent years, for the greater comfort and safety of the signallers, the upper floor windows have been replaced with double glazed units and new metal steps and landing have replaced the wooden originals. New finials, and name boards, present an attractive appearance but, alas, the flaking paintwork will receive no more attention.

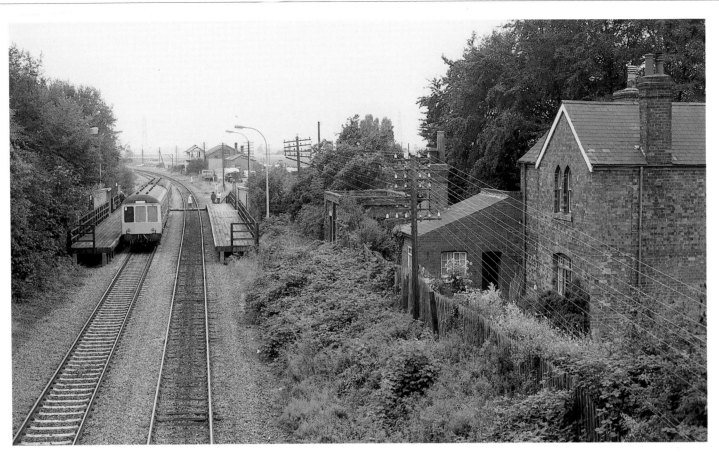

Saturday, 15ᵗʰ September 1984. Ruskington: The circumstances of this station are virtually the same as Metheringham., the re-opening coming a mere 5 months earlier on 5ᵗʰ May 1975. The signal box was a Great Eastern Type 2 and was in services for 100 years before closure in May 1982. A Class 114 DMU calls with the 1230 Doncaster to Peterborough stopping service. Intending passengers and pedestrians were permitted to cross the line here, as no footbridge was provided! *(below)* **Sunday, 13ᵗʰ August 1978. Sleaford North:** The A17 Sleaford By-pass opened up superb vantage point for this location. 47518 cautiously approaches on the line from Sleaford West having called at the station with the 0840 from King's Cross to Leeds. Evidence of the recent singling of this two miles long line is visible to the left of the locomotive. BR installed a facing crossover, just north of the bridge, to enable Up trains to gain access to the remaining former Down line.

(left) **Sunday, 13th August 1978. Sleaford North:** 47519 is signalled towards Sleaford West for a call at the station with an Up diverted ECML train. The surprising lack of a starter signal on the Down will be noted.

(below) **Sunday, 13th August 1978. Sleaford North:** 31318 takes the line to Sleaford West with a breakdown train. The signal box, a GE Type 2, dates from the line's opening in 1882. Of similar vintage is the riding car, a pre-Grouping non-corridor third of unidentified origin.

Sunday, 13th August 1978. Sleaford North: After a signal stop waiting for the previous train to clear the section, 55015 TULYAR is on the move again coming off the Down avoiding line with a railtour heading first to Lincoln (*see also* page 18) before retracing its steps back to here and then via the station en route to the ultimate destination, Skegness. The Down avoiding line had been out of use for many years before resurrection in late 2013 when it became bi-directional.

Sunday, 15th July 1979. Sleaford South: HST 254023 accelerates away from the junction with the 0945 Leeds to King's Cross express as viewed from a foot crossing. Sleaford South signal box is just visible. It was a flat-roof BR replacement in 1957, destined to have a working life of fifty-six years. The connections at this and Sleaford North enabled Joint line trains to use the Great Northern Railway's station.

Sunday, 22nd October 1978. Blotoft: 31254 heads past Blotoft's Up distant lever number 16 with a train of air braked grain hoppers. This was the last remaining GNR somersault signal on the Joint line. However, as a replacement colour light was already in position further away from the box, its days were numbered.

Sunday, 22nd October 1978. Blotoft: 'Deltic' 55008 THE GREEN HOWARDS comes past with the diverted 0915 service from Bradford (Exchange) to King's Cross. The replacement colour light is just visible near the horizon.

Sunday, 22nd October 1978. Blotoft: A rare splash of full sun nicely illuminates the box, which is the standard GE Type 2. Now south of Sleaford, the trackside signs are Great Eastern in origin. A close-up of one of these is shown later. Helpringham, which was between here and Sleaford South, also had a GE 2 type signal box. *(below)* **Sunday, 22nd October 1978. Blotoft:** 37222 heads north with a mixed freight comprising grain hoppers, bogie bolsters, ex MCO 16t wagons and a tanker. The PW hut is a standard LNER design pre-cast concrete structure. This rather remote location once had a short siding for beet traffic situated on the Down side, just south of the level crossing. The only access was via a trailing connection from the Up line.

Sunday, 26th November 1978. Gosberton: 'Deltic' 55011 THE ROYAL NORTHUMBERLAND FUSILIERS is seen with the 1150 service from Leeds to King's Cross. This station was another of the 11th September 1961 closures. The signal box is visible beyond the end of the Down goods loop. This was yet another GE Type 2, which closed in March 2012, being replaced by an interim structure.

Sunday, 26ᵗʰ November 1978. Cheal Bridge, Gosberton: A gleaming 'Deltic', 55007 PINZA has clearly just been released from the Doncaster stable and is seen, without the constraint of a load, galloping south past the signal controlling entry into Gosberton's Down goods loop.

(below) **Sunday, 26ᵗʰ November 1978. Gosberton:** 47421 approaches the level crossing just north of the signal box with a southbound diverted express. Upgrading of the ECML necessitated a programme of diversions in the autumn of 1978. Blue skies blessed this one, but by mid afternoon, the shadows were getting very long.

A SELECTION OF SIGNS

(above, left) **Sunday, 22nd October 1978. Blotoft:** A standard Great Eastern Railway trespass notice, not referring to the Joint line, unlike the GNR pattern signs seen previously at Metheringham.

(above) **Sunday, 22nd October 1978. Mill Green, Spalding:** An early London & North Eastern Railway trespass notice in the style of the Great Eastern Railway.

(left) **Sunday, 26th November 1978. Gosberton:** An LNER 'Beware of Trains' notice probably cast in a former Great Northern Railway foundry, judging by the inclusion of a GNR-style pattern number.

(opposite) **Monday, 6th May 2013. Mill Green, Spalding:** Barriers have replaced the gates, colour lights have replaced the semaphores but otherwise the past lives on in 2013 as DMU 153321 slows for the station stop, just over half a mile away, with the 1441 service from Lincoln (Central) to Peterborough. The typical GE Type 2 signal box, dating from 1882, is in now rather fading Network Rail colours. The box once supervised an Up loop and the outlet from the Down Western goods line, entry to which was controlled by Spalding No. 1.

SPALDING

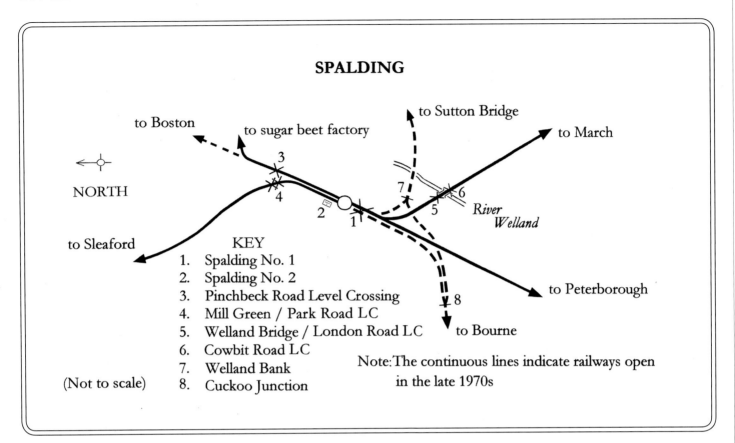

SPALDING

to Boston

to sugar beet factory

to Sutton Bridge

to March

NORTH

3

4

7

6

5

River
Welland

2

1

to Sleaford

KEY
1. Spalding No. 1
2. Spalding No. 2
3. Pinchbeck Road Level Crossing
4. Mill Green / Park Road LC
5. Welland Bridge / London Road LC
6. Cowbit Road LC
7. Welland Bank
8. Cuckoo Junction

8

to Peterborough

to Bourne

(Not to scale)

Note: The continuous lines indicate railways open
in the late 1970s

Sunday, 26th November 1978. Spalding: 'Deltic' 55019 ROYAL HIGHLAND FUSILIER heads the diverted 1000 King's Cross to Aberdeen express through the deserted station (the line would otherwise have been closed on a Sunday) on a bright and frosty early winter morning. The two Up lines extending through the station were from left to right, the line formerly from Boston (main) and the line from Sleaford (Joint), enabling simultaneous arrivals. The trackless bay is clearly visible. Spalding No.2 was switched out hence; the Up starter being constantly in the off position. At its zenith, the station complex, inclusive of the extensive sidings, was 18 tracks wide.

Monday, 6ᵗʰ May 2013. Park Road Level Crossing, Spalding: Unusually for a non-block post 'Manned Gated Box' (MGB), the gates here are left open between trains. The approach of a train is indicated by a bell, which is the prompt for the crossing keeper to close and lock the gates. This indicates to the adjacent supervising block post at Mill Green that the gates can then be locked from there, using the crossing lever, which in turns allows the signals to be cleared, all other factors permitting. Many of the large number of level crossings in Lincolnshire however, have no protecting signals and the keeper is only allowed to open the gates when the on site block indicators show it is safe to do so. *(below)* **Friday, 15ᵗʰ September 1978. Spalding:** A view looking north from the original platform 5. The lifted former bay platform 4 is on the right. A long footbridge spanned all the tracks. Immediately to the north of that was Spalding No.2 signal box, a GN 4b type, closed in July 1984 when the track layout was drastically reduced. Perhaps to avoid confusion between the various local freight facilities, for a while the station name had the suffix of 'Town', but this had by now been dropped.

Sunday, 26th November 1978. Spalding: 47458 heads south with another diverted train. The requirement to serve a sugar beet factory just north of the Pinchbeck Road level crossing had caused the retention of the Up line of the former route from Boston, which had closed on 5th October 1970. Another signal box, latterly named Spalding No.3, had worked the crossing, the gates for which are visible, and the points for the extant Up goods loop. Trains from the Sleaford direction were unable to gain access to the Boston line platform, No.1, and vice versa. On the Down Joint line are the distant and home signals for Mill Green, out of sight, but only a short distance away around the curve. However, Park Road Gate Box is just visible.

Saturday, 12th May 1979. Spalding: It's the day of the annual tulip parade with twenty trains arriving from various parts of England and Wales. In a sharply contrasting scene to that which greeted sister locomotive 47458 six month earlier, 47405 arrives from Newcastle with many of the available lines already full. All the local freight stock had been pushed into the right hand siding for the day. Amongst others, Southern Region based 33053 awaits the return trip to Brighton, while the former Up main provides a refuge for 37091. The service to the sugar beet factory, which utilised this line, was to end the following year.

Saturday, 12th May 1979. Spalding: Trains arrived via the three remaining routes to Spalding. Many approaching from the north continued as empty stock to Cambridge, March or Peterborough for stabling. These included some from the west, which had come across country via the East Midlands. There was some complicated manoeuvring involved for the others. For instance, those arriving from the south proceeded empty to the north end before backing into either of the two Up platforms. The locomotive would then run round, using any clear line, before pushing the stock into a siding or the ex-Up Boston lines, ready for a swift departure in the late afternoon. 31199 (ex King's Cross) is running round. 47411 (ex Hull) has done so and awaits the signal to move off to stable locally on the Down side. In the former platform 5, 37091 has arrived from Southend (Central). Shunter 08133 and a Class 101 DMU complete the busy scene. *(below)* **Saturday, 12th May 1979. Spalding:** 33044 brings the stock of a Ramsgate train forward before backing into an Up platform and running round. A train is clear to leave platform 2 as empty stock. Even the short un-numbered Up bay has been utilised for a DMU. A Class 105 DMU in the erstwhile Down Joint line platform 6 completes the scene. Someone had been busy with white paint on the platform edges!

Saturday, 12th May 1979. Spalding: 47081 ORION is on the Down main, manoeuvring the stock of one of eight trains from the Western Region. The tulip parade originated officially in 1959 as a way of beneficially using the heads of flowers (removed to strengthen the bulb) in the many acres of adjoining tulip fields. However, it was not until the 1970s the zenith of the event that a large number of special trains began to appear. This was an exceptionally busy day for all concerned at Spalding. None more so than the signallers in the two station signal boxes where the work must have been mentally and physically exhausting. The surviving track layout, though no doubt in part retained just for this annual event, had limitations, exacerbating the work involved.

(below) **Saturday, 12th May 1979. Spalding:** All too soon, the early afternoon parade is over. A six-car refurbished Class 114 DMU set departs with a shuttle to Peterborough, as viewed from a convenient footbridge spanning both routes to the south. Several such shuttles ran in addition to the twenty long-distance specials. Poignantly it was announced that the 2013 parade, for which no charter trains ran and which was originally programmed to see the end of many of the signals and boxes illustrated herein, would be the final one. In the face of alleged declining popularity of the event, the two sponsoring Local Authorities cited the cost as the reason.

Saturday, 12th May 1979. Spalding: 47054 approaches from March with the empty coaching stock of a train to go north. The embankment that once carried the avoiding line of the Midland & Great Northern Joint Railway to the south of the town, abandoned on 15th September 1958, is clearly visible. An even sharper curve (track bed out of shot) climbed off to the left to join the M&GN at Welland Bank Junction. There was a corresponding west curve.

Saturday, 12th May 1979. Spalding: 31164 takes the March line with the return working to Acle. The level crossing originally consisted of four tracks, also accommodating lines running in from the quaintly named Cuckoo Junction, the west connection with the M&GN line. As at the north end, there could also be simultaneous arrivals from the south, from two of the four lines, albeit in only certain combinations.

Saturday, 12th May 1979. Spalding: 33053 has drawn forward into platform 1 with the Brighton train. The rarely used former platform 6 hosts another train. As a safety measure, the edge of the former platform 7 had also been painted. This platform became redundant with the closure of the M&GN to passengers on 2nd March 1959. There are still well marshalled crowds waiting outside the station. The railway at its best: shifting large numbers of people to and from major events. *(below)* **Saturday, 12th May 1979. Spalding:** 33053 heads south over the level crossing. From this angle the extra tracks can easily be imagined. In addition to the two lines from Cuckoo Junction, there were sidings and MR goods shed just visible and also a small MR engine shed. A connection from just north of the junction enabled trains from March and Peterborough to gain access to the goods line west of the station. The 'lifted' east chord to the M&GN ran under the second from left span of the footbridge. Freight services from Spalding to east and west over surviving parts of the M&GN system finally ended on 4th April 1965.

Friday, 2nd November 1979. Spalding: On a far more typical, quiet day, one of the original ten 'Peaks' 44007, now bereft of her INGLEBOROUGH nameplates, is signalled into the short Down loop while working light engine back to her home depot of Toton. Earlier she would have worked a train from there to Whitemoor via Syston, Melton Mowbray and Peterborough. Locomotives returning 'light' from March to the East Midlands via Spalding and Sleaford was a common occurrence. Like her nine sisters, this locomotive had spent some time working on the West Coast Main Line but the final transfer, to Toton and a less glamorous life, came in 1962. *(below)* **Friday, 2nd November 1979. Spalding:** A pair of green Class 20s, Nos.20141 and 20143, works a train of 21t hoppers under the station footbridge through the Joint line Up platform (No.2). Meanwhile, the resident Class 08 shunts a rake of General Utility Vans on platform 1. There is little indication that this was no longer a busy station; soon it would change. After 1984, only these two through lines and three small sidings on the northeast side survived. As a refinement, for the greater convenience of passengers, northbound trains were also able to use the right hand nominally Up platform.

Sunday, 22nd October 1978. Spalding: No.1 box was another GN Type 4b which, in addition to controlling the junctions at the south end of the station, also has responsibility for the level crossing with the busy A151 Winsover Road. After the closure of No.2, this signal box was the sole survivor of five boxes in the immediate station area in the station's prime. The Down home signal had a route indicator, in lieu of separate arms, to show the chosen route through the station. The Up junction signal shows the arm for the March line on the right with Welland Bridge's distant below, while straight on is the line to Peterborough. *(below)* **Saturday, 15th August 1981. Welland Bridge:** This GE Type 2 box was situated on the outskirts of Spalding where the Joint line to March crossed two roads and a river. It closed with the abandonment of the line on Saturday 27th November 1982 after 101 years of service. In accordance with normal practice, the official closure date is given as the first day after, i.e. the 28th. Through passenger services had ceased four weeks earlier. Happily, the signal box survives in active use, at a new location, Peterborough station on the Nene Valley Railway.

Saturday, 15th August 1981. Welland Bridge: A Birmingham Railway Carriage & Wagon Company Class 104 DMU approaches the level crossing with Cowbit Road forming the 0935 service from Ely to Sheffield. Spalding No.1's outer distant is below the Down home.

Saturday, 15th August 1981. Welland Bridge: A pair of Class 25s, Nos.25115 and 25126 is typical motive power for the 0835 Derby to Yarmouth passenger service, seen crossing the River Welland. The road vehicles are waiting at the London Road level crossing. On the other side of the river was the second level crossing, for Cowbit Road.

Saturday, 12ᵗʰ May 1979. Postland: General view southwards of the signal box and Up siding. Details of the former station and signal box are as for Cowbit. Like the section north of Lincoln, the route between Spalding and March had been built by the GN. *(below)* **12ᵗʰ May 1979. Postland:** A Class 105 DMU forming the 1238 Doncaster to Cambridge service is passing the box, also anonymous from this end. After the closure of these intermediate stations, passenger trains continued to run non-stop between Spalding and March for a further 21 years before complete closure of the line. As the years have gone on this has become an even greater source of regret as it is now felt that the line could once again have become a strategic freight route.

Saturday, 12ᵗʰ May 1979. Cowbit: Viewed from the former platform, 33044 returns the tulip parade special, seen earlier on arrival at Spalding, to Ramsgate past the anonymous 1882 GN Type 1b signal box, just over 2½ miles south of Welland Bridge. The station here closed on 11ᵗʰ September 1961, a fateful date for so many stations in Lincolnshire, forty years before the date gained worldwide notoriety. *(below)* **Saturday, 15ᵗʰ August 1981. French Drove:** Another anonymous signal box. Were the name boards removed illegally? Signal box and station details are as for Cowbit and Postland. The road here is on the meandering county boundary. Rather illogically, to the northwest is Cambridgeshire, while Lincolnshire is to the southeast!

Saturday, 15th August 1981. French Drove: 31312 with the 0910 Leeds to Yarmouth train on a section of line with Up and Down goods loops. It is hard to believe all this has now gone. This scene is actually just in Cambridgeshire as French Drove, 3¼ miles south of Postland, straddles the county boundary.

Saturday, 15th August 1981. French Drove: Viewed from the signal box, 37048 sweeps past the former platforms with the 0957 from Yarmouth to Manchester (Piccadilly). A Great Eastern sign adds a note of caution. The full title of the station was 'French Drove and Gedney Hill'. Though sunshine here would have been nice, the overcast conditions reflect the mood on a railway, which was by this time doomed.

Saturday, 12th May 1979. Littleworth: Staying south of Spalding, but on the GNR line to Peterborough. This, being the sole remaining line south of Spalding, was also part of the 2013/14 re-signalling and line up-grading scheme. A refurbished six-car DMU set is seen passing with a special in connection with the tulip parade. This line was also closed to passengers as part of the mass cull of October 1970 but in the light of fierce opposition, a limited passenger service was quickly reinstated, on 7th June 1971, with local authority financial support. Regrettably however, intermediate stations such as Littleworth, closed on 9th September 1961, were not reopened. *(below)* **Saturday, 22nd October 1983. St. James Deeping:** A Class 105 DMU is passing with the 16.43 service from Spalding to Peterborough. The circumstances for the station here are identical to Littleworth. This will be the southern limit of the Lincoln Signalling Control Centre's area of operation, fringing Peterborough.

Part Two THE ROUTE TO SKEGNESS – ALLINGTON JUNCTION TO SLEAFORD

Saturday, 30th December 1978. Allington Junction: This is where the direct route to Barkston East Junction and then Sleaford strikes off from the Nottingham to Grantham line about 3½ miles east of Grantham. On 30th September 2005 a brick and pitched roof structure on the same side of the line but the other side of the crossing replaced the 130-years old box in conjunction with the opening of an east to north curve. This had the purpose of taking all local trains away from the East Coast Main Line, as noted in the Introduction. Consequently, this is now designated Allington West Junction. Some services from Nottingham to Skegness omit Grantham, meaning all sides of the newly formed triangle are in regular use. *(below)* **Saturday, 3rd September 1977. Barkston East:** Class 20 Nos.20073 and 20071, with a Leicester to Skegness summer extra, are about to pass Barkston East Junction's distant and soon afterwards go under the East Coast Main Line. Not all the GNR somersaults between here and Skegness were easily accessible but the path to this spot from a nearby lane was well trodden!

Thursday, 29th July 1982. Barkston East Junction: A Class 114 DMU approaches from Barkston South Junction on the ECML with the 1937 service from Grantham to Boston. There was originally a triangular arrangement here with an east to north curve to the ECML at Barkston North Junction. The triangle enabled some interesting permutations. Its most famous use was on 3rd July 1938 when A4 4468 MALLARD and its train reversed from here to the north junction prior to commencing the record breaking run down Stoke Bank.

Thursday, 29th July 1982. Barkston East Junction: A more mundane passage in the form of Class 20s 20141 and 20072, with the 1840 Skegness to Burton-on-Trent is recorded on film. The closure of the signal box was simultaneous with the south to east spur on 30th September 2005. The east to north curve had succumbed in 1972.

Saturday, 3ʳᵈ September 1977. Honington Junction: A typical Lincolnshire scene as a gated level crossing and signal box suddenly appear while travelling on a country road. Situated 1¾ miles east of Barkston East, this was the junction for the line to Lincoln. Though Dr Beeching's report *Reshaping Of British Railways,* published in March 1963, had recommended retention of this for through passenger services and closure of the former Midland Railway line west of Lincoln (St Marks), this was swiftly reversed, closure being with effect from 1ˢᵗ November 1965. The junction signal, with missing arm, was still in situ. *(below)* **Saturday, 19ᵗʰ December 1981. Honington Junction:** It is quite a few degrees cooler as a Class 120 DMU, viewed from the former station platform, passes with the 0954 Skegness to Nottingham service; the station closed on 10ᵗʰ September 1962. Though the junction was located here to allow the points to be worked from the crossing signal box, the line to Lincoln ran parallel for about half a mile before veering off to the north and ultimately Sincil Junction in Lincoln. The crossing's conversion to automatic barriers in July 1984 rendered the signal box redundant.

Saturday, 3rd September 1977. Ancaster: A strengthened 4-car Class 114 DMU set seen with the 1433 departure to Skegness. The station is still open.

Saturday, 3rd September 1977. Ancaster: 47543 passes with the 1330 from Skegness to King's Cross. As well as the original station 'running-in' sign, cautionary GNR signs survived at the platform end.

Saturday, 19th December 1981. Ancaster: A Class 120 DMU arrives with the 0854 service from Nottingham to Skegness. A few modern intrusions only slightly detract from this wintry scene. The box survives, for a few more winters at least. *(below)* **Saturday, 3rd September 1977. Rauceby:** Signal box with station beyond, seen from the west. The signal box, a GN Type 1 dating from 1880, is situated on bridge No.5 over the infant River Slea, as indicated by the bridge number sign - an unusual attachment to a signal box. Like Ancaster, this station remains open.

SLEAFORD

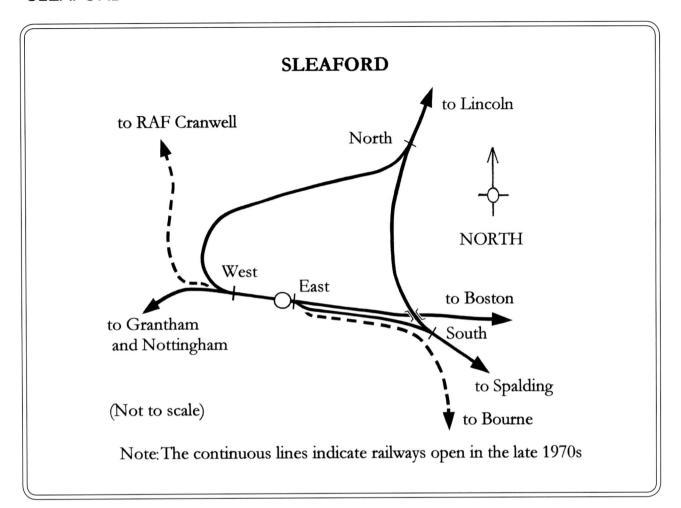

SLEAFORD

to RAF Cranwell

to Lincoln

North

NORTH

West

East

to Grantham
and Nottingham

to Boston

South

to Spalding

to Bourne

(Not to scale)

Note: The continuous lines indicate railways open in the late 1970s

Sunday, 15th July 1979. Sleaford: Class 25 Nos.25309 and 25318 approach with an unidentified excursion to Skegness. The station was in full bloom and the surviving goods shed also adds to the attractive traditional railway setting.

Sunday, 15th July 1979. Sleaford: Having just traversed the curve from Sleaford South, 'Deltic' 55011 THE ROYAL NORTHUMBERLAND FUSILIERS arrives with the diverted 0840 King's Cross to Newcastle express. It will make connection here with a shuttle DMU to Grantham in lieu of the scheduled stop there. BR only resorted to buses when unavoidable!

(above) **Sunday, 13th August 1978. Sleaford West:** 47544 comes off the link from Sleaford North in order to call at the station with the 1205 service from York to King's Cross. BR had singled that line the previous year and pending a more satisfactory arrangement, trains went on to the Up main before immediately using the (normally) trailing crossover to reach the Down main prior to entering the station.

(right) **Sunday, 13th August 1978. Sleaford West:** A miniature GN somersault signal still controlled the outlet from the siding. The signal box is from 1882 being GN Type 1b. Like its neighbour Sleaford East, it was not included in the 2013 closure programme. The box controlled the outlet from the once quite extensive goods yard and a small engine shed. Following the opening of a branch to RAF Cranwell in 1917, which increased the workload, the GNR extended it to accommodate 57 levers. This private branch had a short-lived passenger service, which ended in 1927. It closed completely in August 1956.

Sunday, 15th July 1979. Sleaford: It is not apparent from this view, but as we have seen, this was a busy day for Sleaford as there were the East Coast Main Line diversions in addition to the usual quota of seasonal extras to Skegness. The signal box is identical in age and design to Sleaford West. It now enjoys Grade II listed status being part of the traditional railway scene here. At this time BR 'modern image' signage name boards unfortunately disfigured it. Signs more sympathetic to the original have now replaced these. The colour light signal that gave equal priority to the diverging routes towards Boston and Spalding has been likened to a well-known cartoon character! *(below)* **Sunday, 15th July 1979. Sleaford:** Another 'Deltic' 55012 CREPELLO is arriving with the 0830 Hull to King's Cross. The station is full with 37054 on the 0840 Cambridge to Skegness preparing to back down to Sleaford West having run round its stock (see page 3) and a Class 114 DMU with the Grantham shuttle on the so-called Local line serving Platform 3.

Thursday, 23rd September 1982. Sleaford: A Class 114 DMU arrives with the 1031 Doncaster to Cambridge service which will run via the, by now, doomed line from Spalding to March. It looks like some maintenance is taking place. Health and Safety standards have certainly improved for the better in the last 30 years. *(below)* **Saturday, 8th September 1984. Sleaford:** 40086, seen earlier passing Gainsborough (Lea Road) returns anonymously with the 1324 service from Skegness to Manchester (Piccadilly). This longstanding summer train had become a virtual weekly railtour by his stage, mainly due to its rostered Class 40 haulage.

BOSTON - SLEAFORD

Saturday, 28th August 1982. Heckington: A Class 114 DMU arrives with the 0845 service from Nottingham to Skegness. The windmill, dating from 1830, is the only surviving eight-sailed windmill in the country, having been restored to full working order in 1986. The Heckington Village Trust has since restored the wooden shelter on the Up platform.

Sunday, 13th August 1978. Heckington: A quiet moment on a Sunday afternoon. The Eastern Region totem seen on the wall was a notable survivor at this late stage. The station buildings had been saved by the Heckington Village Trust from demolition in 1975 and a small, but interesting, railway museum, complete with two model railway layouts, is now located in the former waiting rooms. *(below)* **Saturday, 28th August 1982. Heckington:** Class 20 Nos.20157 and 20172 pass with the 0850 from Leicester to Skegness. By this time, BR had singled the line between Sleaford East and Heckington and the start of the single line section is clearly visible. The signal box, a GN type 1b, dates from 1876 and, like the station, remains open.

Saturday, 28th August 1982. Heckington: A Class 114 DMU arrives with the 1516 to Nottingham. The Up outer home, seen in the distance, plays a significant role in protecting the single line section ahead if the section is occupied, as it is quarter of a mile in the rear, the standard margin of overlap in semaphore signalled areas. This double track oasis from Hubberts Bridge is just less than eight miles long. *(below)* **Saturday, 28th August 1982. Wyberton:** 20157 and 20152 are seen again, this time passing the GNR signal box which had closed as a block post in May 1981 after 77 years service when the section between Hubberts Bridge and Boston was singled. It survived as a crossing box until December 1983.

BOSTON

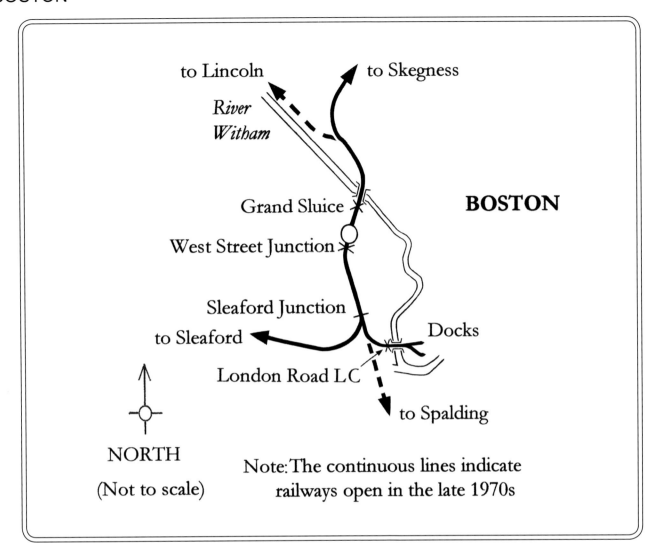

to Lincoln   to Skegness

River Witham

BOSTON

Grand Sluice

West Street Junction

Sleaford Junction

to Sleaford

London Road LC

Docks

to Spalding

NORTH

(Not to scale)

Note: The continuous lines indicate railways open in the late 1970s

Saturday, 28th August 1982. Boston: Diesel-mechanical shunter 03034, out-stationed from Lincoln, is captured in the sidings south of Broadfield Lane. This is in the vicinity of Sleaford Junction where the Sleaford line diverged from the main line continuing on south to Spalding. The branch to the docks goes off to the left in the far distance. There were formerly Up and Down goods lines to the east of the main lines, between here and West Street Junction. The closure of the Peterborough to Grimsby line as a through route on 5th October 1970 reduced Boston from main line to branch status at a stroke.

Saturday, 28th August 1982. Boston: '20s' 20180 and 20135 enter with the 0922 train from Derby to Skegness. The imprint of the lifted sleepers for the Up and Down main lines can still be discerned. The dark blue Eastern Region 'running-in' station signs at each end of the station were rare but very welcome survivors at that time.

(above) **Saturday, 28th August 1982.
Boston:** Class 20 Nos.20180 and 20135 have to wait for 'Peak' 45059, hauling the 1100 service from Skegness to Sheffield, to clear the 4½ mile single line from Sibsey before they can proceed further. They will be underway just as soon as the signallers at Grand Sluice and Sibsey have done their work.

(right) **Sunday, 13th August 1978.
Boston:** Grand Sluice signal box, which was located at the northern end of the station. From the date of some rationalisation in 1924 until the closure of the line to Coningsby Junction in 1963, it had control of East Lincoln Junction about a quarter of a mile to the north. The box closed in November 1985 after 104 years service. In the background is Boston's most famous landmark, the tower of the church of St Botolph, 272½ feet high and better known as 'Boston Stump'.

Saturday, 28th August 1982. Boston: Class 40 No.40061 passes through in stately fashion with the 0818 service from Manchester (Piccadilly) to Skegness and all is well with the world. As at Lincoln (Central), the platforms originally had substantial roofs that extended over the platform lines. Removal came during the 1960s with replacement by relatively easily maintainable, if less elegant structures. *(below)* **Saturday, 28th August 1982. Boston:** The Grade II listed West Street signal box is now Boston's sole surviving block post and is a GN Type 1 dating from 1874. Behind it, rather appropriately is a GNR Gresley high roofed secondary vehicle which dated from around 1907, latterly in Departmental use.

Saturday, 28th August 1982. Boston: Class 31 No.31242 approaches the station with the 0921 from Leeds to Skegness. Between 1848 and 1852, when Boston was on the Great Northern Railway's main line from London to the north, the GNR established a locomotive works behind the GNR vintage vehicle seen in the background. With the opening of the more direct 'Towns Line' through Grantham, Newark and Retford, the more conveniently located works at Doncaster was established and the rest, as they say, is history. *(below)* Saturday, 28th August 1982. Boston: Looking northwest, we see a Class 120 DMU with the 1131 service from Skegness to Nottingham which can prepare to proceed now that 31242 has cleared the single line from Hubberts Bridge. The junction signal in the foreground clearly once carried a signal on the missing doll. It was, to the Up goods line, which diverged immediately beyond the two-track level crossing.

Saturday, 28th August 1982. Boston: '20s' 20135 and 20180, standard motive power for the 1258 passenger service from Skegness to Derby, await the signal to recommence their journey.

Saturday, 28th August 1982. Boston: Another returnee, 31242 with the 1330 Skegness to Leeds. This telephoto view emphasises the void left by the removal of the fast lines. The conversion to single track at Grand Sluice box is evident in the distance

(above) **Saturday, 28th August 1982. Boston:** 40061 passes through again, with the 1320 return working from Skegness to Manchester (Piccadilly). The track bed of the centre roads has been used to good effect to house the raised flower beds.

(right) **Saturday, 28th August 1982. Boston:** The branch from the docks, looking west from the bridge over the River Witham. Somersault signals and an attractive octagonal gate box mark the crossing of London Road. The vertically separated arms are an alternative way of signalling a diverging route in non-main line situations: left to right, reading from top to bottom. Happily this branch is still open. In the 13th century, the port here was England's second in status, only London was ranked higher.

Saturday, 28th August 1982. Boston: A four-car Class 114/105 DMU combination arrives with the 1224 working from Nottingham to Skegness. Broadfield Lane crossing box is just visible through the haze of the late summer afternoon. Road vehicles are parked on the former goods lines and sidings, however former engine shed and works buildings still defiantly dominated the skyline. *(below)* **Saturday, 28th August 1982. Boston:** The Class 105 end of the Nottingham train. These passengers have no cause to regret the loss of the original roof to the footbridge. Had Dr Beeching's proposals been carried out this would have been the end of the line and the train would be making a swift return west rather than continuing on to Skegness.

BOSTON - SKEGNESS

Saturday, 1st September 1979. Maud Foster: The delightfully named signal box and crossing keeper's house were situated approximately 1½ miles north of Boston station. The box dated from 1877 and functioned as a block post until the conversion to single track in April 1981. We are now on the East Lincolnshire Railway, which remained a separate company until Grouping in 1923, though wholly operated as part of the Great Northern Railway.

Saturday, 28th August 1982. Maud Foster: 31161 works the 0938 King's Cross to Skegness after the reduction to single track. The box remained as a crossing box until June 1985. The name is of a 16th century local landowner who is more permanently commemorated by the working five-sailed Maud Foster windmill in Boston and, less glamorously, a drain, which the train is just about to cross.

Saturday, 1st September 1979. High Ferry: The ground level signal box is of GN Type 1b design and was in use from November 1890 to April 1981. No doubt over the years countless signallers were grateful for the lack of steps when performing their crossing gate duties! Sibsey's Down distant is located below the home signal.

Saturday, 1st September 1979. High Ferry: 31122 rushes past, towards Skegness, with empty coaching stock. Being the weekend after a bank holiday, and the last before the end of the school holidays, perhaps explains the need for a relief train to assist the reluctant exodus from the popular resort.

Saturday, 1st September 1979. Sibsey: It was not just on the East Midlands trains that Class 20s appeared. This pair, Nos.20071 and 20159, passing the site of Sibsey station, are heading the 0747 service from Sheffield, albeit via Nottingham. The station closed on 11th September 1961.

Saturday, 1st September 1979. Sibsey: This 1888 signal box is happily still in use as a block post. The current single line section from Boston reverts to double track just north of the crossing and remains as such for the remainder of the route to Skegness.

Saturday, 1st September 1979. Old Leake: 31188, with the 0800 Leeds to Skegness, is passing a 1903 replacement box which was developing a pronounced lean! Use as a block post continued for a few months longer, until May 1980 and thereafter as a crossing box, until February 1989.

Saturday, 1st September 1979. Old Leake: A view looking east taken later in the day. The crossing had the usual compliment of Great Northern Railway signs. The station here which was on the left closed earlier than most on this stretch of line, on 17th September 1956. The road authority has subsequently straightened out the kink in the road.

Saturday, 1st September 1979. East Ville: The Type 1b signal box opened in April 1889 but became a non-block post in April 1973; full closure came in March 1989. Like Sibsey, the station here had closed on 11th September 1961.

Saturday, 1st September 1979. East Ville: '20s' 20171 and 20194 approach with the 0922 Derby to Skegness train. A GNR bridge number plate adds to the usual collection of GNR railwayana on display.

(opposite) **Saturday, 1ˢᵗ September 1979. Bellwater Junction:** '31' 31227 powers past with the 0838 from Chesterfield to Skegness. This was one of the loneliest boxes on the GNR system and was the junction for the line from Lincoln, 32 miles distant via Woodhall. This had closed in October 1970, with the exception of the nine-mile section from Lincoln to Bardney which lingered until 1983 for freight traffic. The locomotive marks the spot where the line curved off to the right.

(opposite, bottom) **Saturday, 1ˢᵗ September 1979. Bellwater Junction:** 47409 heads the 0912 from King's Cross. The leading vehicle appears to be a Royal Mail TPO. Was it commandeered as a luggage van in the absence of something more suitable?

(right) **Saturday, 1ˢᵗ September 1979. Bellwater Junction:** The friendly Signalman gave permission for a little exploration. This is the Down home signal. The junction was 11¼ miles north of Boston.

(below) **Saturday, 1ˢᵗ September 1979. Bellwater Junction:** 40112 runs past with the 0814 from Manchester (Piccadilly). Surprisingly, since the road over the adjoining crossing is only for farm access, the box, a GNR Type 4a from 1913, is still open.

Saturday, 1st September 1979. Little Steeping: A view of yet another Type 1b signal box. It enjoyed a working life of just three months short of a century of years, closing in March 1989. Like most of the others on this section of line, the station closed on the fateful 11th September 1961. The East Lincolnshire Railway formerly ran to Grimsby, but the line to Skegness veers off to the right at the site of Firsby South Junction, 1¾ miles north of here.

(below) **Saturday, 1st September 1979. Thorpe Culvert:** 47532 heads away with the 1232 Skegness to Leicester. Unfortunately, there was no better opportunity to capture this location with the somersault Down home signal. 'Topping and tailing' which would have helped, was not then widely practised! In 2003 Network Rail replaced the very badly leaning 1899 structure with a new brick and pitched roof box. The replacement is remarkably sympathetic to the traditional design. The station here, on the Skegness branch proper, remains open.

Saturday, 1ˢᵗ September 1979. Wainfleet: 31227, seen earlier at Bellwater Junction, returns with the 12.50 service from Skegness to Sheffield. The signal box, like all the other intermediate ones on the branch is of Type 1b design and dates from 1899. It remains open and has recently acquired Grade II listed status. A footbridge, with separate steps for both station users and pedestrians held up by the gates, was situated just this side of the level crossing. The canopy on the Down platform was still standing, but was looking rather the worse for wear! *(below)* **Saturday, 1ˢᵗ September 1979. Wainfleet:** A few minutes later 20194 and 20171, somehow missed on their outward journey, round the curve with the 1258 Skegness to Derby. A group of ladies await a local train to the seaside. The railway opened for goods traffic as far as here on 11ᵗʰ September 1871, passenger services commencing six weeks later.

Saturday, 1st September 1979. Wainfleet: A refurbished Class 114 six-car DMU set, forming the 1245 from Nottingham, is just less than five miles away from its destination. The telephoto lens brings the Down somersault distant signal into view. The station once boasted a goods shed and a very small engine shed. *(below)* **Saturday, 1st September 1979. Havenhouse:** A Class 120 DMU leads a refurbished pair of Class 114s to form the 1034 service from Nottingham. At that time, the railway was able to respond swiftly to peak levels of demand to strengthen such services.

Saturday, 1st September 1979. Havenhouse: Just three miles into her return journey, '40' 40112 passes somersault home signals on both lines with the 1322 working from Skegness to Manchester (Piccadilly). The 'modern image' signs and lights only very slightly detracted from the scene at the third and final open station on the branch. The signal box closed in March 1989. *(below)* **Saturday, 1st September 1979. Seacroft:** Being a mere mile from Skegness (seen in the distance) and serving nowhere nearby in particular, strangely this location once had a station. It closed on 7th December 1953. The platforms were tiny and occupied no more space than the extent of the freshly cleared area seen on the left hand side of the track. The signal box, which lived on as a crossing box after ceasing to be a block post in 1967, survived in this role until April 1990.

Saturday, 6th August 1983. Skegness: There is an air of expectancy as 40013, without her long-removed ANDANIA nameplates, arrived with the 0801 from Manchester (Piccadilly). Happily, this locomotive lives on in preservation.

SKEGNESS

Thursday, 8th March 1979. Skegness: A 'route survey' trip to Skegness found the terminal to be predictably deserted and rather bleak, with summer still some months away. Seen in a rare flash of brightness, the partly covered platform 4 is hosting a Class 114 DMU with the 1558 to Nottingham. At that time platforms 2 to 6 were still in use, the track having been lifted from the outer face of the most northern island, which once adjoined a turntable. The station opened on 28th July 1873, being the catalyst for the expansion of Skegness from a village, population 500, to a fully-fledged seaside resort.

(below) **Saturday, 6th August 1983. Skegness:** 45113 waits with a short Mk II rake forming the 1237 service to Leicester. The outward working had arrived at Nottingham behind Class 25 No.25262. Normally this would be a Class 20 or Class 25 double-header with Mk Is; so clearly there had been problems back in the East Midlands. A Class 120 DMU also waits departure time, in platform 3.

Saturday, 6th August 1983. Skegness: Some passengers are clearly relishing the prospect as 40013 commences the return journey to Manchester (Piccadilly) at 1320. No.31134, in platform 7, will have a further 76 minutes to wait before heading off to Leeds. The listed Grade II signal box is a GN Type 1 of 1882, extended to 80 levers in 1900. Evidence of the extension at the country end is clearly visible from this angle.

Saturday, 6th August 1983. Skegness: 31134 arrives with the 0921 from Leeds. Meanwhile 40013 had run round her train in the carriage sidings and will shortly reverse the rake into the station. In the halcyon days, there was also a matching set of slightly longer carriage sidings on the left hand side of the line with the additional facility of a triangle, situated approximately opposite the visible milepost 9, to turn larger steam locomotives than the turntable could accommodate.

(below) **Saturday, 6th August 1983. Skegness:** 31134 is now backing into the carriage sidings to run round and then reverse back into the station. Having already completed this manoeuvre, 40013 awaits the 1320 departure time.

Saturday, 6th August 1983. Skegness: 47482 leaves with the 1300 service to Derby. The absence of Class 20s on both this and the Leicester service on this day was quite exceptional.

Saturday, 6th August 1983. Skegness: West to east! One of the Brush Type 4s the Western Region named in the 1960s, No.47086 COLOSSUS awaits departure from platform 5 with the 1535 service to Peterborough.

Saturday, 7th July 1984. Skegness: Eleven months on and normal order is restored as 20213 and 20217 are seen backing out with the stock of the 0816 from Leicester.

Saturday, 7th July 1984. Skegness: 20217 and 20213 stand in the deserted looking station with the 1158 return working to Leicester.

Saturday, 7th July 1984. Skegness: The departure board.
Excluding the trackless platform 1, only platform 2 is without an allocated train.

Saturday, 7th July 1984. Skegness: On this occasion the Manchester train arrived without its customary Class 40 motive power. '37' 37030, an able deputy, is reversing the stock back into the station.

Saturday, 7th July 1984. Skegness: 31187 arrived with the 0900 from Leeds, some 71 minutes late! In the distance can be seen the Up Starter and Down outer home. The latter was a quarter of a mile in the rear of the station throat. Thus, a train could be accepted from Havenhouse even if a conflicting movement was taking place in the station. The single-armed home signal with no route indicator is unusual in not informing drivers into which platform they have been routed, though the 10 m.p.h. speed restriction is common to all, so there are no safety issues.

Saturday, 7th July 1984. Skegness: Viewed from a conveniently located foot crossing, 31187 finally departed with the 1433 to Leeds, 25 minutes late as a direct consequence of the late arrival. Skegness grew on the arrival of the railway. The Great Northern Railway, using the now legendary Jolly Fisherman poster designed by John Hassall, promoted Skegness to strengthen its popularity beyond the East Midlands - its natural hinterland. This endured through several generations, but, alas, busy summer Saturdays as depicted here are now a memory.

Acknowledgements

David Allen and John Hooper of Booklaw.

Dave Harris - for permission to quote from his Midland Microcosm study.

Andy Knowles - for his professional insight.

Hayden Reed - for assistance throughout.

Cathryn and Paul Thacker - for the benefit of their local knowledge.

Bibliography

An Illustrated History of Great Northern Railway Railway Signalling - Michael A. Vanns - OPC

Beeching The Inside Track - Robin Jones - Mortons Media Group Ltd

Branch Lines around Spalding Michael Black Middleton Press

Lincolnshire Industrial Heritage - A Guide - Editor Neil Wright - published by Society for Lincolnshire History and Archaeology

Passengers No More - G.Daniels and L.Dench - Ian Allan

Railways of Lincolnshire - Paul Anderson - Irwell Press

Railways to Skegness - A J Ludlam - The Oakwood Press

Railway World (various) - Ian Allan

Signal Box Register Vol 3 LNER (Southern Area) - Signalling Record Society

Steam Days (various) - Redgauntlet Publications

The East Lincolnshire Railway - A J Ludlam - The Oakwood Press

The History of the Great Northern Railway - Charles H Grinling - Methuen

The Lincoln to Grantham line via Honington - A J Ludlam - The Oakwood Press

The Railway History of Lincoln - J. G. Ruddock and R.E Pearson - J. Ruddck Ltd.

Sunday, 26th November 1978. Gosberton: In the lengthening shadows of the November afternoon, HST 254010, then nearly new, provides a sharp contrast with the steam age setting all around as it heads for the north, having departed King's Cross at 1300.